HOW TO USE A PLANNER
without wasting time

A Busy Mom's Guide

MYSTIE WINCKLER

To Elaine Lortz

my first homemaking accountability friend

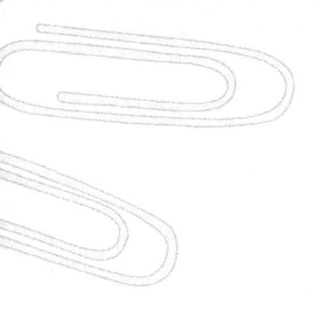

Get the accompanying
free planner printables at
ConvivialPlanner.com

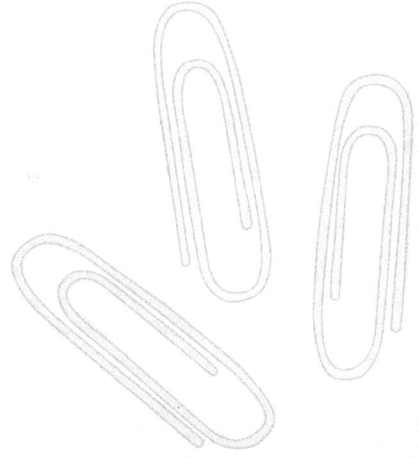

CONTENTS

Introduction 9

SECTION 1: GETTING STARTED
1. What is a planner? Why do I need one? 14
2. Putting together a planner 19

SECTION 2: ESSENTIAL PARTS OF A PLANNER
3. Your goals and the big picture 29
4. Your calendar view 35
5. Your meals strategy 41
6. Your routine details 47
7. Your weekly dashboard 52
8. Your running lists 57
9. Your project hub 63
10. Your daily card 68

SECTION 3: HOW TO USE A PLANNER
11. Using your planner 75
12. Your weekly review 81
13. Regrouping with your planner 88

About the author 94

INTRODUCTION

I have spent hundreds of dollars on planners. I have a large box full of every conceivable office supply product that might help with getting things done. I have spent hours – perhaps hours totaling days – setting up apps to help me track what I should be doing when.

Back in the day, when I was a young wife with only babies and toddlers, there was no social media. However, there were forums and blogs. I read and followed several, picking up tips and tricks and ideas that really did help me figure out how to manage myself and a household better.

One popular practice at the time was a household binder. There were instructions, templates, and examples available online. We could turn a three-ring binder into a household reference, instruction manual, and data center.

I started with a full-size 1 1/2-inch binder, but I needed a free hand to carry it because it wouldn't fit in my purse, and it took up so much space in my diaper bag that there was hardly any room for diapers. After all, the whole point of the binder was that it was always with you, so you'd have whatever information you might need right at your fingerprints.

Next I created a half-size household binder. It fit in my purse, and I used it much more often than the full size one because it also fit on a handy spot on my kitchen counter.

I made a grocery store price list, and "important numbers" reference page full of phone numbers for emergency services I never used. I wrote the sizes of my two little boys, crossing off old numbers and updating it every three months as they grew and grew. I began honing my master pantry list and menu planning routine that became Simplified Dinners.

One day, as I lugged the infant carrier into the grocery cart, rummaged for my binder, and made sure my keys landed in my purse, I directed my toddler to hold onto the side of the cart as I shopped. My binder had to go up in the toddler seat area of the cart, after all, or else I couldn't reference my price book and be sure I was getting a good deal.

And that was the last day I used my household binder. It had become just one more hassle in an already full-of-hassle outing, and it was expendable.

I have no regrets about the time I put into making that binder. Over the years I made a few half-hearted attempts at trying less cumbersome iterations. There was the year I had a Palm Pilot that I thought would be the solution, but what effort it saved in size, it ate in time. We were late to adopt smartphones, but I did have an iPod touch for a number of years that renewed the digital organizer itch. Between those devices I had half-size binder planners, clipboards, post it notes, and index cards. In all my attempts at creating a complete planning system, I didn't try a preprinted designer planner until I was nearly 40. I had always hated the thought of having pages in a planner I didn't use, and I loved the flexibility of adapting my planner to what I wanted to track at the time.

Yet, with flexibility comes a curse. I probably spent more hours designing my own planner pages than I ever spent using them. As soon as I didn't work my planner, I started not by returning to what I had already set up, but by starting from scratch with a new template.

Now, that wasn't all wasted time. In a lot of ways, putting together and filling out a planner is half the benefit. The exercise of setting up a planner allows us to wrap our heads around what's going on in our lives and in our heads. We see all the pieces as we write them out and gain clarity in the process. But if we get only half the benefit of a working planner, it is still an ineffective use of time.

We claim that other half by using it daily. Somehow, it's the hard part, even though it takes less time and thought. Using a planner boils down to looking at it and updating it as we go.

Why is that the hard part?

Because it takes follow-through. We're bad at follow-through, and that's exactly why we need a planner in the first place.

In this short book, I'm going to walk you through the process of setting up a planner that works without wasting our time. This process works with any purchased planner, self-designed planner, or digital planner. I know it will work, not only because of all the planners I've set up for myself over the last twenty years but also because for the last 5 years I've walked through the process with hundreds of other ladies and seen dozens of creative applications.

We don't need the perfect planner to make us organized. We need better habits. We need a streamlined, simple system, not an elaborate and perfect one. Then we need to use it.

As we set up our planner through this guide, we'll also build the habits it takes to follow through, not only with our planner, but also with our plans. Those habits also must be simple and streamlined so we can do them on less than ideal days. Also, we don't want to plan on life going smoothly just because we now have a planner.

Planner or not, good habits or not, we will get thrown curveballs in life. We will get derailed. We will fall off the bandwagon. We will lose touch with our plans. So we also need to learn how to get back on track quickly after seasons of survival mode without feeling like we have to go back to square one.

Planners and great systems do not make life go our way. If that's our goal, we'll be perpetually frustrated. We don't need to make life go according to plan. Instead, we need to help ourselves respond and adapt to life as it unfurls with calm, cheerful goodwill.

A good planner helps us respond well to real life by short-circuiting our response to overwhelm – if that's the approach with which we set it up and use it.

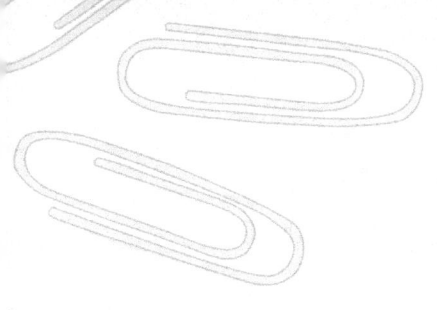

SECTION 1

Getting Started

"In preparing for battle I have always found that plans are useless, but planning is indispensable."
—Dwight D. Eisenhower

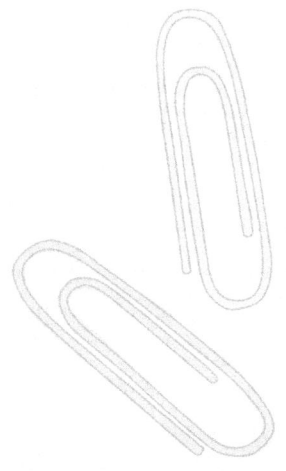

1

WHAT IS A PLANNER?
WHY DO I NEED ONE?

The best way to waste time on planners is to shop for them. Not only are there product pages to browse and photos to examine, but there are blog reviews and YouTube videos galore promising to help us make a more informed decision so that we can end up with the right planner.

Back before I started homeschooling, several older homeschool moms all had the same advice when I asked them about curriculum: Almost any curriculum will work if you do. The curriculum isn't what matters the most in your homeschool. Whether or not you actually use it and do the work is what really matters. No curriculum works automatically, on its own. And it's the same with planners. Almost any planner will work if you do. Just like curriculum, a good planner can help us get more done with less stress. It can help us stay on target and not get lost in the weeds of distraction and overwhelm. But it's not the pages themselves. It's us using our planner, whatever it is, that makes a difference.

The planner itself never does any of the work.

Because we are the ones actually working, not the planner, we should spend less time browsing for the perfect planner and more time practicing the habits that will make any planner a useful tool in our lives.

Those habits are twofold: Looking at the plan and choosing the next best thing to do.

A planner is a tool to help us recognize what the next best

thing to do is. We use it to keep track of information and responsibilities so that our minds are not clogged with details that spring to mind exactly when we don't need them. With those details safely stored in a clear home, our minds are then free to think and respond without overwhelm.

We often shop for planners with the underlying assumption that having an organized planner will make us be more organized.

However, it's really the other way around.

When we are organized, we use a planner in an organized, effective way.

Being organized is about being prepared and ready for the day. When we're organized, we do what must be done with cheerfulness and grace.

Organization is not about matching containers with cute labels. Productivity is not about squeezing the most out of every day. We get organized and increase our productivity because we want to be good stewards of our time and energy, investing it in people. We have to remember we're not machines cranking out widgets and trying to increase our efficiency, judging our success by our output.

Instead, we look at how effective we're being in the callings God has given us. How are we investing in our relationships, first with God, then with our husband, then with our children, and rippling outward from that central base to the broader community? How are we exercising responsibility and care with the resources we've been given, including our homes, income, land, and technology so that they are available for kingdom use, not means of self-indulgence?

If we move through our days on default mode, we're going to thoughtlessly slip into self-centeredness, swayed by social media and our own sinfulness to consider only our own comfort as we decide what to do moment by moment.

When we evaluate ourselves as if we are widget-making machines, we decide organizing the pantry was a waste of time because it didn't stay organized and photoshoot-ready beyond two days. However, when we recognize our job as caretakers – as homemakers – we see that the value of organizing the pantry isn't the end product but the reality that the task helped us manage the food and supplies we have with increased knowledge and wisdom.

When we assume we're supposed to have the same efficiency and productivity as a machine, we get frustrated with laundry and dishes and meals because there's never a finish line. Imagining ourselves as machines, we feel like it's just a treadmill, getting us nowhere. We want a conveyor belt, factory life where there's a result at the end to tally and "count" as finished.

However, that's not how we or the world were created to run. Adam and Eve were created in a garden and told to tend and keep it – before the Fall. Tending and keeping, along with worshiping, fulfills our original job description as humans. So our repetitive work at home that is a frustration when we compare it to an industrial measure of productivity is actually a satisfying joy when we see it in light of our original mandate of fruitfulness.

We shouldn't set out to use our planner to minimize work the world has told us is demeaning so that we can maximize me-time. There is no true fulfillment, satisfaction, or joy there.

Instead, we use our planner to tackle our work with zeal.

When we manage our responsibilities and ourselves well, we do end up with more time to focus elsewhere. A well-maintained home will take less time to keep up, but a chaotic home tackled haphazardly will require more time and attention and increase the burden in other aspects of our lives.

When we can't find what we need, trip over clutter, and feel low-level stress because we know we can do better, everything else also becomes harder.

A planner helps us get more of the right things done because it's easier to keep track of things when they're written down. We can arrange our work efficiently so our efforts are not scattershot and haphazard.

However, when we sit down with a planner, we tend to let wishful thinking take over. If it fits on the paper, it will fit in real life, right? We know that's not true, but we do it anyway. The truth is that the more we put into our planners, the less likely any of it will happen. If we have to visually and mentally sort through the plan whenever we look at it, we're defeating the purpose of writing it down.

The purpose of a plan is to beat decision fatigue. When our thinking is clear and our resolve high, we write down as a note to our future self what ought to be done when. If we can't trust those notes or if those notes take extra effort to decipher, then it's just another obstacle and not a help at all.

A planner will help us be organized and effective if it only takes a glance at it to remind us of what's on our plate and what we should choose next.

Planner clutter is worse than clutter in the closet or cupboard because it means the planner can't do its job. So we must restrain our temptation to include all the things on a single planner page. Instead, we ought to only add what we are truly responsible to do.

Then, when we feel overwhelmed or scattered, a look at our planner clears the cobwebs and puts us on the right path forward. We must keep our plans simple, so they are easy to read and understand at a glance.

On the flip side, planners need to be adaptable because life changes on us. We can't plot out our week in a planner page and then just make it all happen. That never works because that's not the way life works.

Through a combination of overplanning, overzealous expectations, and unforeseen life circumstances, our plans end up being infeasible. We need to be able and willing to adjust and tweak them as we go.

Keeping a planner will not make us magically be able to do it all. However, when we use a planner that lets us see our life responsibilities at a glance, we will be able to use our time more wisely and effectively.

The pages and the practices lined out in this book will help you not waste your time with wishful-thinking plans or unnecessary information. We'll work through the exercises that make our planners containers of relevant details and build the habits that make us diligent, attentive women.

Let's get started.

2

PUTTING TOGETHER A PLANNER

Setting up a new planner can seem daunting. We wonder if it's even worth the time. After all, we have all put countless hours into setting up systems, planners, trackers, apps, and checklists before, and here we are, still scattered and scrambling.

But a working planner does save more time than it takes, as long as we don't waste time in wishful thinking instead of real planning. How we use the planner, what we put in it, and when we look at it matters more than which templates we use or brand we buy.

Templates and styles and designs can vary greatly, and although there are variety and differences, most planners have the essentials that you need to keep it effective and useful:

- A summary of your current goals or big picture
- A list of your current projects
- A calendar with at least the next 3 months available
- A weekly view
- A spot for your daily top 3
- Space for taking notes and keeping running lists and thoughts

So how do you choose your planner? Simply pick one you find appealing that has room for these six essential pieces.

The perfect arrangement of pages will not change you, so you don't need to examine each and every planner possibility that exists. Instead, you should choose a planner that you're attracted to. After all, the more time you spend with it, the better it will work (to a point – but we'll cover that, too). If you have a small bit of affection for your planner, you'll be more likely to use it and more likely to come back to it after a time of neglect.

Choosing a planner and figuring out what you like will take some experimentation. Your first pick doesn't have to be your final pick. But you should commit to your planner as an experiment for about three months in order to get a feel for the process and your actual preferences.

Three months is enough time to learn lessons from your experience with the planner. It's enough time to let the newness factor wear off and make it through the slog weeks after the planner isn't perfect anymore. It's enough time to give the planner – and your habits – a chance.

If, after three months, you think something else might work better, do a brain dump. List out what you did like about the planner. List out what you didn't like or what you wished worked better. Brainstorm about what might help you more. Do you need more habit tracking? More list space? More calendar space? More space for your week or more space for each day?

Don't go planner shopping or printable browsing until you've thought about what you and your current situation needs more of and less of. Don't shop or browse for the perfect solution, because you won't find it. Perfection-hunting wastes so much time.

It can be hard to remember alternative options for planners, too. A planner doesn't always come hardbound and preprinted. There are many creative ways to keep a planner, and none of them are better than another. What makes each one work is the person working it.

So start an experiment. Evaluate after your experiment. Adjust as needed.

The five kinds of planners

We need to remember to think outside our conventional boxes and know our options when it comes to planners. Sometimes what used to work stops working for a variety of reasons, and something totally different is what we need to break us out of our slump.

The following are different materials available for creating workable planners. As we discuss the different elements we need inside our planners, each chapter will have a section for ways to set it up within each of these five different methods.

Preprinted Planner

A brand new, blank planner hot off the shelf (or fresh out of the box) seems to hold infinite possibility. The blank spaces are not so blank as to leave you spinning your wheels. There are prompts to help you fill the planner with all the right, inspirational things.

Some will cajole you into tracking water by printing water droplets on each day's plan. Some will emphasize habits and give you space for twelve. And if the planner has twelve spaces, doesn't that mean I have to choose twelve to make the planner complete?

We might spend an hour or two filling things in, excited for the fresh start and the promise of change. Then we discover that an hour or two isn't even enough time to adequately prepare the planner and all its prompts and blanks it gives us for a complete life plan.

You might not need all the prompts a preprinted planner has. Washi tape can affix a printed verse or motto over any pages you don't want to use and don't want to feel guilty for leaving blank. Post it notes on the inside cover can add extra flexibility if you aren't sure where something should go at first.

Often, the biggest hang up we experience with a preprinted planner in all its glory is the fear of messing it up. We don't like our handwriting. We might misspell something. We will change our plans after inking them into the week – and then what?

Then there's white-out tape or there's simply rolling with the punches, crossing things out and scribbling over the top. Our planner will end up reflecting our life if we're actually using it. We might want to pretend our life is smooth and beautiful and always goes according to plan, but that's our pride whispering temptations that will prevent both real faithfulness and true beauty.

Keeping our planner pristine isn't an indication of an organized or productive life. It's just an indication that we want to hold on to our perfectionism and a fake self-image.

Life is messy and so our planners will get messy, even beautiful preprinted hardbound planners. You're not ruining your planner or messing up your organization when you make a mistake or when you alter course in a day or a week or a month. You're simply using your planner, which is what it is for.

Find the list of our community's current top 5 pre-printed planners and why we like them with example photos at ConvivialPlanner.com – and click "see community examples."

Self-bound Planner

Some of us are hard to satisfy. We don't want anyone else to decide what should be in our planner because no one else knows our life and what we need like we do. So every week we reinvent our planner. After all, finding and printing new pages might just be the key to our plan actually working this time. Right?

Nope. When you're putting together your own planner, you really need to emphasize sticking with what you put together for a while before tweaking or changing your pages. You can always add in blank note pages as needed to brainstorm and get on paper what you need, but it's so easy to waste time adjusting documents when what we really need is just to do the work.

As you choose your binding for your planner, don't forget to add blank note pages, especially if you're spiral binding it yourself or having it printed and spiral bound at an office store. It's easy to forget blank note pages, but having one place where we can write anything and everything down is one of the key pieces that makes a planner helpful.

Whether you use a disc-bound planner, a three-ring binder, an old-school Franklin Covey cover, or any other system, you'll want to have your own hole puncher available that will let you insert what you need into your planner. Also, consider adding a folder insert to the back so you can stick in mail to send or checks to deposit or other papers you want to keep with you.

Find the list of our community's current top 5 binder options and why we like them with example photos at ConvivialPlanner.com – and click "see community examples."

Clipboard Planner

Another way to keep your planner pages is on a clipboard or padfolio. Without a cover like a bound planner, it's easier and simpler to lay eyes on the plan – no opening and flipping required. A clipboard is super flexible for keeping whatever papers you need in whatever order is most convenient at the time. The clipboard makes it easy to write on your pages on the go, as well.

Another possibility that I categorize as a clipboard approach is a preprinted planner pad. A weekly-view planner pad might be all you need, especially if used in a padfolio to help it be more sturdy and portable.

Some of our members inside Simply Convivial Continuing Education love using white boards, too. This approach is also similar to the clipboard because your plan is right on top, visible at a glance, no need to open and flip. If you need a highly convenient, flexible, and visible planner, a paper-sized whiteboard might be a great option to try.

Bullet Journal Planner

The bullet journal is another way to create your own planner, but without the need for a printer. You can choose the size and binding and paper weight you prefer. You can find blank, lined, or dotted pages and almost any color or design you want.

However, with so much versatility and so many options, bullet journaling can become a big time sink. It's often more fun to watch videos of people setting up and using their bullet journal pages than it is to actually set up your own.

It's more fun to design and draw new pages than use the ones already set up.

I recommend setting a timer for your page-design time, which will need to be weekly. Start with a basic set up within that designated time and then add extra doodles, color, or stickers in any leftover planning time or in spare moments throughout the week.

Don't wait for your design and your doodles to be perfect before jumping in and actually using the pages you set up. It's not the template itself that makes the planner work, after all; it is you, using it, that makes it work.

Our community examples at ConvivialPlanner.com include top notebook brands and example photos of other women's bullet journal applications.

Digital Planner

Our phones are an incredible tool in our pocket, but we frequently use them mostly for distraction.

However, because our phones are powerful tools of distraction with apps designed to cultivate addictive tendencies, using our phones for productivity is fraught with peril. To make our phones a tool of clarity and focus, we have to be intentional and consistent or else we'll be pulled into the time-suck that is scrolling.

Because smartphones do have so much potential, it seems a shame to not utilize them. We can have all our life information at our fingertips, always within reach of our powerful pocket computers.

There are real benefits to writing things out by hand, but there are also real benefits to having everything on our phone. It is possible to use it as a very effective planner, especially when we utilize notifications and reminder pop-ups as an external reminder system.

No planner needs to be a single, all-or-nothing type. We can effectively mix and match paper and digital options based on our habits and needs and preferences.

Conclusion

As we develop our planner system and our planning habits, we'll draw out applications for all five of these methods of keeping plans. You can always head to ConvivialPlanner.com and click on "see community examples" for up-to-date linked lists of the best apps and digital tools and examples of mixing and matching.

Planner organization can seem complicated, but it really doesn't need to be.

Any planner will work if you use it daily.

However, we do have to actually choose a planner and get it up and running before we can use it daily.

Find the resources page with updated links and recommendations for these different planners at ConvivialPlanner.com and click "see community examples."

SECTION 2

Essential Parts of a Planner

"Unless commitment is made, there are only
promises and hopes; but no plans."
—Peter F. Drucker

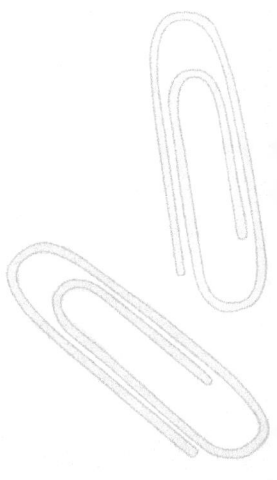

3

YOUR GOALS AND
THE BIG PICTURE

We have a lot on our plates; it is true. That's why we're committed to getting a working planning method. We can't juggle it all in our head.

When we try to juggle it all in our head, we begin to feel flustered, scattered, overwhelmed, and pulled in too many directions. Sometimes even when it doesn't look like I'm drowning in my home, I am still drowning in the chaos in my head.

And sometimes when the house looks chaotic, it's actually because I'm doing ok in my head and following through on my real current priorities. Sometimes the state of the house is just not where the focus needs to be for a time.

To climb out of the chaos that threatens to sink us inside our own emotions and thoughts, we need perspective. We need a clear view above the fray. What is the big picture and where are we in it?

Much of the productivity and planning advice out there claims that the perspective we need is a vision for a 5-year outcome. When we as mothers at home try to do that, we are rather at a loss. We don't even know how many children we'll have in 5 years. If your oldest is 5, you can't accurately foresee what it's like to have a 10 year old – and the same is true if your oldest is 10 and you're trying to predict 15 or 15 trying to predict 20.

We have to put one foot in front of the other where we are, and not get too wrapped up in predictions and visions. We should have a general direction, but we don't know how that will play out – and we don't need to know how it will play out.

Rather than try to shoot for some 5-year outcome or vision, we should have a general purpose and direction and then make a short-term plan that aligns with a faithful purpose and direction.

Progress doesn't begin with an imaginative vision. Progress begins with small steps. Of course those steps must be in the right direction to be actual progress, but you don't need a life mission statement or articulated vision to know what's most important now.

If you know you need to lose weight, you don't need to decide a goal weight or imagine what life will be like when you're thinner to begin eating less and moving more. Most likely, any goal weight you set at the beginning will shift as you approach it, either up or down. Knowing the precise end is not required to make good next decisions.

In the same way, you don't need annual goals, much less life visions, to make an appropriate action plan for your real day to day and week to week. Look at the actual responsibilities in front of you, make a plan to tackle those first, and the next phases will become clearer as you begin to move forward. Most planners available ready-to-go in stores and online begin with a goals section of some kind. Perhaps they direct you to write very formulaic SMART annual goals or perhaps give you space for a more artistic sketch of a life vision.

If you have done the work and have goals or focusing statements you believe will help you make better plans, then by all means include them here in the opening pages of your planner.

However, if you don't have such big picture plans in place already, just skip it until the more granular parts of your planner and your decision-making is in order. You will not miss out, and any big picture plan you end up with later will be better for having first dealt with the immediate needs in your life and home.

After all, our desire here is to not waste our time planning, and the reality is that the farther out you plan, the more time you will waste planning because situations will shift and plans will have to adapt.

When we begin by looking at weeks instead of years, we won't be able to waste time with unrealistic, grandiose goals. In January it is easy to let the overachiever in us all be the one in charge of writing goals. By contrast, a short-term perspective forces us to examine where we are now and what we can reasonably expect of ourselves right now.

The only big picture plan you really need to remain effective in your planning is a calendar kept up to date at least two months out and a list of your current, active projects. Both of these key elements of a good plan will be covered in future chapters. I'm not saying you should never have big picture goals or visions, but rather that planning at that level is not the best place to begin. When planners open with a section for goals, it implies that the first step of setting up a planner is writing goals.

Writing big-picture goals is not the first step to setting up an effective planner. If you start there, you're likely to waste a lot of time in speculation rather than actual planning.

However, if you do already have goals written or big picture plans made, then by all means include them in the front pages of your planner. After establishing basic planner habits, it can be helpful to evaluate each section to iterate and improve your approach. As you do, you might find you are ready to do some bigger picture thinking and writing.

When you have a big-picture plan, it does belong at the beginning of your planner, because those serve as reminders of your direction and priorities that will filter into your weekly plans as needed.

Even though they aren't essential in order to begin, it is important to have a home for those big picture plans when you do make them. Keeping plans and priorities written on paper and reviewing them, rather than trying to keep it all in our heads (and spinning round and round mentally), is key to calming the overwhelm that looms as we juggle many needs and responsibilities.

As life unrolls, we need reminders of what's important and what we ought to be focusing on. And also, as life unrolls, we will need to amend and adapt our goals and plans. No big picture plan will ever be set in concrete. We'll need to update and revise our goals not only because life changes, but also because we learn more as we work.

In your planner

Whatever kind of big picture goals or boundaries you've written out for yourself – if you have any – should come near the front of your planner where you can read and reread them regularly as you flip through your planner.

- PREPRINTED PLANNER – Most pre-printed planners will come with goals pages or blank pages up front. If they don't, you can add sticky notes over other front matter pages or use washi tape to secure a new page over pages in the front you aren't using. Alternatively, you can use a notes section in the back; just add a flag as a tab to make them easy to find and review.
- SELF-BOUND PLANNER – Some of the opening pages in your own planner can be dedicated to your goals or priorities, whether you use a form or not. When you flip through your planner, it's good to have them in a convenient spot to review.
- CLIPBOARD PLANNER – Goals, projects, and priorities don't warrant being on the top, most visible space of a planner, but they are still valuable to have written out to review regularly. Of course you can include a page on your clipboard, but you might also use a whiteboard clipboard and have them on the base or backside of the clipboard itself.
- BULLET JOURNAL PLANNER – Your goals and big picture spread is a great place to get creative because it will be relevant and reviewed for as long as you use the notebook and it won't need to change much. If you love adding doodles, watercolor, or stickers, this is a great spot to do that. Spending time adding artistic touches to the goals spread is one way to remember and think about those goals.

- DIGITAL PLANNER – Your goals and the big picture can have their own note if you're using an app like Evernote, or they might be a project themselves in a task management app. Another idea is to make a graphic as your phone background with your goals or big picture. The key is keeping them someplace where there are not too many taps before you can review them.

You can find photo examples of big picture goal pages in each of these kinds of planners at ConvivialPlanner.com – just click "see community examples."

4

YOUR CALENDAR VIEW

Your calendar is your #1 productivity tool to keep track of life.

Let me tell you how I know.

There was that time I was driving home from piano lessons in the middle of the afternoon when it suddenly struck me that I'd signed up to take a meal to someone. When was I supposed to take that meal? It was coming up, wasn't it? Yeah. It was that day . I was supposed to show up with a hot meal for a family in two hours.

I had known, of course, that I should have put it on the calendar. I had intended to put it on my calendar. I just forgot – clearly.

Write it down, right away – in a place where you'll see it. I have missed doctor's appointments because I hadn't put it on my calendar. I have missed online meetings I made because I didn't look at my calendar (or I looked at the wrong day). I have gone through my day blithely, happily believing I had no obligations only to have my Google calendar audibly ping me 10 minutes before I was actually supposed to be somewhere. It was on my calendar. I just hadn't looked at it.

We must not let our failures with our calendar habits and time management and self regulation prevent us from working on improving all three. Improvement is possible and it is also gradual.

When we get the organization overhaul itch and buy a new planner, a new app, a new book on how to do it Right, we are often hunting for the overnight solution, the fast fix.

Starting with your calendar will give you the fastest fix, but it will not be a total transformation. The reality is that our problem as humans is not primarily a knowledge problem. Simply knowing what we need to do is not enough. We then have to do it, and a vast array of factors continually complicates the execution of our plans.

In addition to our calendar, we need to cultivate the habit of getting back up after falling down, whether the fall was self-inflicted, sinful, or circumstantial. Failing our system is not an excuse to stop trying but rather an opportunity to learn and grow and try again.

Improving your calendar habits will have ripple effects on every aspect of your organization and management. Better calendar routines will trigger further productivity improvements. It is the best place to get started.

Even if you don't have any of the other planner pieces described in this book, if you keep the following five calendar rules, you'll be organized enough to be effective.

Calendar Rule #1: Keep all appointments and only appointments on the calendar.

If you've made a commitment to someone else to be somewhere or do something at a particular time, it should be on your calendar.

Don't assume you'll remember. Put every appointment – even sports practices or regular club meetings that you think you'll never forget – on the calendar. These are not clutter; they are reminders that your time is spoken for.

Eliminate any actual calendar clutter. Calendar clutter is any non-obligation or anytime-commitment on the calendar. These should be on a to-do list, not on a calendar. Our calendars should be an at-a-glance chart of how much time you have available to you, in what chunks, each day.

Your calendar needs to be trustworthy. Don't put your hopes or wishes on your calendar. If you add things you hope to get to in a day, you'll have to mentally sort and decide every time you look at it, which will make you not want to look at it. Keep your calendar reserved for real appointments.

Calendar Rule #2: Keep one master calendar.

If you have appointments and birthdays and other commitments spread around on multiple calendars, you'll need to look at more than one in order to know what's going on. The more places you have to look, the more likely something will fall through the cracks.

Keep one master calendar so you have only one place to look – one trustworthy place that holds everything you've committed your time to and every date-bound data point you need to have available. You might have more than one calendar – like a meal plan or sports schedule taped to the fridge – but make sure you keep one master calendar with everything on it up to date and accessible.

Calendar Rule #3: Always Take your calendar with you.

In order to keep your calendar up to date, keep it with you always. Add appointments and commitments to it immediately as you make them. Then you will never wonder whether or not you're forgetting an appointment.

Calendar Rule #4: Sync your calendar with your husband's.

Staying on the same page with your husband is easier when you are in tune with each other's calendar. My husband doesn't want to see everything on my calendar, and I don't need to see his work calendar, but for appointments and obligations outside his work day, it's helpful to know what's on the family schedule. We do this by sharing Google calendars, but a weekly conversation about what's on the calendar is a good practice, also.

Calendar Rule #5: Look at your calendar a minimum of Twice every day.

A calendar will do you no good if you don't look at it. Build time into your day, at least in the morning and the evening, to look over your calendar for the day, the week, and the month coming up.

Your calendar is a way of keeping track of your time-sensitive commitments. If you need to be somewhere or do something at a specific time, it needs to be in a spot where you will remember the time of that obligation.

Whether it's a doctor's appointment, a coordinated phone call, a lunch date, or a gym class, you need to see the landscape of your day, of your available hours, by looking at your calendar. Our calendars tell us what time is already spoken for. They show us what we need to prepare for. They give us the hard lines within our days.

Without a trustworthy, accurate calendar, we stare at a day planner or out the window, trying to remember if there was anything else we needed to do that day. We miss appointments or scramble at the last minute. We double-book ourselves or have to bail on a friend because we forgot about the orthodontist appointment.

But when we have a complete calendar, we know our commitments and can make plans confidently.

The calendar is the organizational tool we should begin with. Before we set up apps or elaborate task management systems or decorate plans with stickers, we need to have a working calendar.

In your planner

Having an accurate calendar that you can always have on hand and actually look at is key to being prepared and organized.

Many people successfully merge a paper planner with a digital calendar, which works especially well if you always keep your phone on you but don't want to always carry your planner. A family wall calendar doesn't count as your master calendar because you can't carry it around. It's a good tool for family communication, but you should populate it from your own personal calendar.

- PREPRINTED PLANNER – Most purchased planners include a calendar because keeping track of our obligations is the most essential part of keeping a planner. If a digital calendar is your master calendar, consider using the pre-printed calendars for after-the-fact journaling and recording of life.
- SELF-BOUND PLANNER – You'll want to print month-view calendars at least three months out and keep these toward the front of your planner. It's also nice to have a year at a glance available for looking up particular dates or circling special days.
- CLIPBOARD PLANNER – Your weekly plan will likely be the top page, but your calendar, perhaps printed double-sided, should be right behind it.
- BULLET JOURNAL PLANNER – a die-hard handcrafted bullet journal will draw out the calendar pages early on in the notebook, but another option is to print calendar pages and tape them in. You can even make it a fold out calendar if it's sized and placed well.
- DIGITAL PLANNER – Google calendar or iCalendar are common apps that sync with a variety of services; you can also set it to send mobile notifications or email summaries to help with reminders to look at your calendar, which is ultimately what makes any calendar work.

You can find photo examples of big picture goal pages in each of these kinds of planners at ConvivialPlanner.com – just click "sample pages."

5

YOUR MEALS STRATEGY

Dinner is one of the most important family times we have every day, but often we go into it harried and exhausted. After a hectic day, we can hardly get food on the table because we have no energy left.

A menu plan is supposed to solve that harried feeling, but somehow our efforts rarely seem to pay off. We must be missing some menu planning magic.

What we're actually missing, however, is how simple it's supposed to be. Getting meals on the table is a complex project, but our menu plan should be a tool we use to streamline and simplify the process.

All kinds of issues complicate our food decisions and needs. Allergies, sensitivities, health considerations, and pickiness limit our options. If we have too much repetition, everyone grows tired and bored with the meals that are supposed to bring connection and fellowship.

Even if we've made the menu plan, we have to make sure the right ingredients are on hand at the right time. Plus, even with a plan, we still have to actually make the meals, which always takes more time than expected.

Removing options is often the best way to simplify. Limitations and boundaries speed up our cooking capacity because many decisions are off the table. Removing options removes decision-fatigue.

Decision fatigue is real. A menu plan should simplify getting meals on the table because it reduces the number of decisions we have to make on the fly. However, if we add more decisions and more contingencies to the plan in an effort to set up the perfect plan, our plan will crash and burn – and so will we. Dinner doesn't have to take a lot of concentration if we put boundaries around our choices and use templates to make planning and preparing simpler and smoother – and therefore faster.

Getting dinner on the table involves coordinating a lot of moving pieces. Having a meal plan and master pantry or grocery list as an integral part of our planner is key to combating a scatterbrained, overwhelmed approach. But meals are worth the effort because they are a key part of our family's connection time.

Your menu plan might be a specific list of what will be served when or it might just be a list of options to pick from each day. However, no menu plan will work unless our grocery shopping lists and habits are coordinated with the plan.

You can do that by shopping first, buying what's on sale, then planning your meals after the haul is home. You might write out your shopping list while planning and then schedule a shopping trip appropriately. Another option would be filling an online shopping cart as you menu plan and pick it up or have it delivered before you need those ingredients.

Whatever the strategy, there are three menu plan pieces to keep in a planner so that it is useful – eliminating decision fatigue and streamlining family meals.

First, start by making your Meals Strategy page. There are many ways to do this, but the key is to have notes of options to choose from and a pattern to use weekly as you plan. You can create a strategy week to week, month to month, or even 6–12 weeks at a time. I also like to keep these plans on file so I can reuse the ones that work well the following season.

For example, if you decide to have "Chicken Monday," your Meals Strategy page might have a list of 3-4 kinds of chicken meals. The same goes for "Taco Tuesday" or "Crockpot Wednesday" or "Beans & Rice Thursday" or "Pizza Friday." Perhaps "Chicken Monday" should be followed by "Stir-fry Tuesday" to use up the leftovers. Making a resource page in your planner allows you to think about the best flow and to work within smart constraints when you menu plan for the week.

You can also list ingredients you'll need to keep on hand to make these meals happen. How many pounds of chicken should you buy each week? How many pounds of potatoes or beans? The start of your grocery list happens here, so each week it takes very little thought or preparation to put together the complete list.

Or, perhaps you want to think about it the other direction. What do you already have on hand in your freezer or in your pantry that you ought to use? List those, and then make meal plans around what you already have stocked.

Sometimes I will even add a list of the vegetable sides. I'll plan to do a salad twice, glazed carrots, roasted broccoli, and roasted brussels sprouts – but I won't necessarily do them always on the same day of the week. This way I know what veggies to buy, we get variety, and I don't have to stare blankly into the fridge (as much).

Second, include a master pantry list or a master grocery list – whichever fits your way of thinking and planning. What do you buy regularly and want to keep on hand? Do you know about how much of each you go through in an average month? Tracking this and noting it in your planner helps you keep a stocked and efficient pantry and also keeps you from "stocking up" on items that might be on sale but that you never actually use.

Third, indicate on your weekly overview what meals you actually select (or, at least a short list of options) for that week. Knowing what we're going to feed people is a key part of our action plan. We make our weekly plan not from scratch each week, not from browsing recipes, but by referring to our strategy page.

We also need a standard way of keeping (and place to keep) a running grocery shopping list. I often keep my shopping lists on a Post-it on whichever of these meal pages I'm referencing. I can pull it out at the store and not carry in my whole planner. I can easily pass it off to my husband or teen. Then I can toss it and replace it with a new one after it's been shopped.

As we gain experience and practice menu planning and grocery shopping, we'll pick up our own preferred patterns. We'll get better at using what will go bad quickly first and using the shelf-stable pantry meals later. We'll collect family favorites and keep those ingredients on hand. We'll learn what we can do to turn leftovers into another family meal. Meal preparation can be both simple and satisfying as our skill increases.

In your planner

There are so many meal planning templates out there. As with other templates, any of them will work if you do, so don't worry too much about the format. Simply choose one that helps you think through your own family's needs and resources better.

- PREPRINTED PLANNER — Few ready-to-go planners have a place for meal and pantry strategizing. A note page section in either the front or the back, tabbed with a colored flag can do the trick to help manage feeding our people.
- SELF-BOUND PLANNER — When you put together your own planner, a benefit is that you can create a menu section that fits your situation and the way you think it all through. Take that advantage, keep the information together, and know that it will take a few iterations to work out something you like.
- CLIPBOARD PLANNER — A page on your clipboard with your master grocery/pantry list and a meal strategy on the back will pack a heavy punch without bulk or weight to your portable planner.
- BULLET JOURNAL PLANNER — A temptation of bullet journalers everywhere is to overcomplicate the layout and add more than is needed. Start small and add only as it becomes helpful.
- DIGITAL PLANNER — You can put your menu plan on your digital calendar so you can drag and drop and repeat meals easily; if you do that, make another calendar in a different color that you can easily turn on and off and consider setting a reminder to prompt you when you should start cooking rather than when you

should start eating. You can also put your meal strategy in your notes app or task app, as well.

You can find photo examples of menu plan configurations in each of these kinds of planners at ConvivialPlanner.com – just click "sample pages."

6

YOUR ROUTINE DETAILS

I am always trying to turn over new leaves. Too many times I've tried turning them overnight, and instead I've fallen on my face.

My leaves of change are not actually new, fresh, spring leaves like I imagine, but old, dead, crunchy winter leaves that shatter into a million pieces when stepped on. Those "new" leaves are actually shriveled and crispy because they're not connected to the tree of reality.

My "turning over a new leaf" plan, whether it comes at the start of the year, the beginning of the school year, my birthday, or just the Monday after I hit some internal crisis moment, is never realistic.

My written plan lays out what to do to keep everything up to par, doing all the things with aplomb. On paper, it looks doable. I have a strategy. I have checkboxes. If I did all the things, I'd be on top of it.

Sometimes on that first Monday it is possible. But then Tuesday will be a wash and Wednesday will be a drag. So I go back to the drawing board to spend more time creating yet another new and improved plan.

If I were to base this plan on reality instead of my vain imaginations of doing all the things, I would start with where I am and my next step, not with a plan that reflects what I think would create an ideal future.

Making an awesome planner doesn't make a new life or a new self at all. So instead of creating a complete system that you think will work perfectly right out of the gates, begin and build a system of routines slowly, improving and adjusting the plan after a few weeks of actually working with it.

When our systems don't work, our first instinct is often to make a new plan – to begin again fresh on Monday. But that's a sure way to waste time and spin our wheels while feeling productive. It's much easier to move checkboxes around in a file than to just spend 10-15 minutes working, especially when we know that the job cannot be completed in 10-15 minutes.

Yet, we might be surprised. Ten or fifteen minutes is usually enough time to make visible progress, even if the job isn't finished in that time. In the end, we'd get a lot more done and stay on top of the chores and details of life if we took advantage of 5, 10, and 15 minute pockets of time in our day.

After all, too often we fritter such margins away by checking social media, flopping on the couch, or wandering aimlessly around the house. Such choices diminish our energy and attention overall, dragging us down right at the point where we could be moving forward.

Those short bits of time are perfect for routines. Unless we're operating with the whack-a-disaster game plan (and sometimes that's legitimately where we're at), most of our housework should fall under the routine category – regularly recurring work, regularly done. Routines are the approach that allow us to address our home responsibilities without feeling like we're always responding to emergencies.

You will want to track completing your routine on your weekly dashboard so that what needs to be done is on your most visible, most visited page. However, because there will be so much on that page, you'll want abbreviations and shorthand there. Perhaps you did your morning routine on Tuesday, but how can you be sure unless you know exactly what constitutes your morning routine?

The Routine Details page is where you track the components of your various daily and weekly routines. Outlining it all on one resource page allows you to see the big picture and know where you have room to scootch in another task or discover what's missing in your method.

Whatever you do, don't begin a Routine Details page by thinking about the best, most complete set of routines, writing them out, and then thinking you have identified a way to keep house perfectly. Instead, start with those routines you already have in place.

Then, think about what one piece of your daily and weekly duties really needs to be improved next. Add it to a currently existing routine or add in a new routine, tied to something that already happens regularly. Cues like "after lunch," or "after school," or "before snack" work well because we're aligning our routines with the natural, existing flow of our household.

It takes time & effort to implement a routine, but once established, the routine decreases the amount of time and effort needed to maintain it. The key is to not try to revamp your whole life at once, but to start one by one, going slowly but steadily through your routines.

If you need a bit more guidance with this process because you aren't sure how to climb out of survival mode and daily chaos, the 6-week course inside Simply Convivial Continuing Education called Sweep and Smile will help you tackle your own current state and set up doable weekly routines customized to your family.

A household run on routine and good habits is beautiful and worth the effort. A household that runs on routine takes less thought and effort than the household that does not. Routines give us the rhythms that remind us to keep up our good habits.

In your planner

Your weekly dashboard will likely have abbreviations and cues for your routines, but not what makes up each routine. Somewhere in your planner you need your routine reference, and that's the job of this section.

- PREPRINTED PLANNER – Like your menu strategy, your routine details will likely need to be in the back of the planner in the notes section because there's not room for it with the front matter. Flag it so you can review it at least weekly and remember what you ought to be doing when.
- SELF-BOUND PLANNER – When you put together your own arrangement of pages, you can decide whether you'd prefer this reference page in the front or back; feel free to experiment with different placements to see which spot is easier to review for you.
- CLIPBOARD PLANNER – Although you can certainly have an extra page clipped on your board just with your routine details, you might also consider printing it on the backside of your weekly dashboard page so

that all you have to do is flip it over to see what exactly each routine ought to include.

- BULLET JOURNAL PLANNER – Just as with the self-bound planner, you can choose where to put your routine details in your bullet journal; be sure to keep them clear and straightforward without too much adornment so that they're easy to comprehend at-a-glance for review.
- DIGITAL PLANNER – Two approaches work equally well with a digital planner; first, you might simply make a note in a note taking app with the details; second, you can create repeated tasks in a task app for your routines and put the details in the description so that if you aren't sure exactly what you must do to check it off, you can click and see the full list.

You can find photo examples of routine detail pages in each of these kinds of planners at ConvivialPlanner.com – just click "sample pages."

7

YOUR ROUTINE DETAILS

I am sure we've all been there before. We make a grand plan and then life gets in the way and we're left floundering and flying by the seat of our pants anyway.

It's an easy trap to think that because that happens so often, planning is a waste of time and an exercise in futility.

But it's not true.

One military saying is "No plan survives first contact with the enemy." That's what we experience in home life also: No plan survives first contact with a real day. However, generals don't stop planning because of this fact and neither should we.

When we plan, we are not determining how life is going to happen. We plan so we know our options and our priorities, so we understand what is and isn't feasible, and so we are prepared to adjust and flex in the midst of real days unfolding unpredictably before us.

After all, it's easier to roll with the punches life throws when we have a plan to adapt than if we're approaching the week aimlessly and cluelessly.

Even when plans don't play out the way we expected, having a plan guides us. Often, it's our own lack of mental and emotional energy hindering progress and motivation. A plan also reminds us of that direction we're trying to move toward. The process of planning itself is useful to us. The fact that we have a plan is indicative that we've thought through where we want to go and how we will get there. Our thinking-through and writing-down informs the intuitive choices we make when we meet life as it happens.

Your planner might have a lot of moving pieces, but the workhorse, the essential piece, is the week-at-a-glance view. Keeping a weekly dashboard – in any format – will help you keep your plates spinning when life is hectic and busy. The weekly dashboard is the workhorse of your planner.

Think of that image of a workhorse as you set up and use your dashboard. When we imagine a particular planner or page in the planner as being the heart, the key, the important piece, we become paralyzed as we stare at it. We don't want to mess it up. Something that's so vital ought not be scribbled on.

Thus, what ought to be vital is dead to us for lack of use.

A weekly dashboard, by the end of the week (and maybe even at the beginning), will be a messy page because it will be a reflection of real life. Our job as both mothers and planners is not to contain life into neat and tidy baskets, but to orchestrate many moving pieces – that means mess happens. Mess is part of the plan or our plan is a waste of time.

Your weekly dashboard is where the hands-on orchestration of all the details happens. It is your at-a-glance, go-to overview. What details make it onto the weekly dashboard will vary from situation to situation and person to person, but there are three universal components.

First, your dashboard needs boxes for each day with plenty of room for writing. What you write in those boxes might change from week to week, but there will usually be day-specific yet non-appointment notes to track. For instance, if I plan overnight bread for Friday's dinner, I need a place for a note to start that bread on Thursday.

Second, your weekly dashboard needs a spot for tracking your home's necessary routines and any habits you are currently trying to build. After all, our sense of our own consistency is often inaccurate. Especially with mood or hormone swings, we can feel one moment like we're doing pretty well and the next like we're totally failing. Instead of relying on our feelings, a routine and habit tracker gives us concrete data to evaluate not only how we're doing but also where we most need improvement.

Third, you'll want to choose a weekly set of top three tasks. There's always a lot on our plates and many tasks to track, but this section is where you call out what really matters most and can't be skipped this week. Choosing a limited number of priorities – not huge projects - helps us accomplish more because we stop procrastinating on the tasks that matter most. Much of our mental and physical wheel-spinning happens when we're avoiding important tasks. Calling those out and then knocking them out helps us become people who follow through, people who keep their commitments.

The weekly dashboard is the plan of action. We don't know how each day will play out, but we do need an idea of what needs to get done when. So we make a weekly plan to move our current projects and commitments forward – not a moment-by-moment, play-by-play plan, but a weekly overview.

Then when available time pops up amid all the hustle and bustle of life at home, we know what we need to do.

The whole point of working the plan is that we can know what we have on our plate so we can be both focused and flexible. Knowing what our responsibilities and duties are and listing what we've chosen to prioritize in those cool, reflective planning moments will help us be engaged in the present moment and make better decisions on the fly as life actually unrolls. We can roll with the punches and adapt on the go.

Our weekly plan – more than a daily one – banishes aimlessness and brings clarity and momentum. So no matter what kind of planner you keep, you need a weekly dashboard.

In your planner

You'll update and populate your dashboard during your weekly review. Then, every morning and evening, review and update your dashboard again. This is the page to keep open and visible during the day so you can continually refer back to it.

- PREPRINTED PLANNER – Although there are some planners made with only month and day views, the vast majority have a weekly spread available. That's the page you need to evaluate when you're picking a planner to see if it will help you track what needs to be tracked in your own life. Most planner pages will have some spot for habit tracking, but drawing your own in or adding them via post it note also works.
- SELF-BOUND PLANNER – Be careful not to spend too much time browsing Etsy for printables or designing your own; it's so easy to get sucked into the hunt for the perfect that we forget we won't know

what works until we get started. A blank page and some quickly sketched boxes is just as likely to work as a fancy print design.

- CLIPBOARD PLANNER – The same warning for self-bound planners applies here; to begin to experiment, you could even use post-its on a piece of cardstock to discover what you need and like and will use. The post-it method also works on whiteboards or the front (or inside) of a kitchen cabinet. Think more about visibility than design when you first begin keeping a weekly dashboard.

- BULLET JOURNAL PLANNER – Every week you get a chance to draw a new weekly spread, so you can iterate faster. However, try not to start from scratch each week. The more familiar you get with your spread layout, the more convenient and useful the dashboard will become to you.

- DIGITAL PLANNER – If you are using a notes-based app like Evernote, then your weekly dashboard is a note that needs to be starred and in your shortcut bar so that it becomes the default note to open. Although many task apps try to give you a weekly view option, they typically don't function as dashboards; it'd be better to use the weekly view as a reference during your weekly review.

You can find photo examples of multiple weekly dashboards in each of these kinds of planners at ConvivialPlanner.com – just click "sample pages."

8

YOUR RUNNING LISTS

There's no doubt we're spinning a lot of plates in our lives, trying to keep things from falling apart. However, we usually try to do this spinning all in our heads. This causes a lot more stress than we realize.

Our minds are not the best reminder system. They are much better used for thinking, processing, deciding, and creating. When we use our minds as a container for reminders, then there's not enough space in there for creative thinking – sometimes not even enough left for simply being present in the here and now.

Whether we do it on paper or digitally, we need to keep reminders of our various tasks to manage them. These task lists can feel overwhelming the longer they get, but if we know how to mentally categorize and emotionally handle them, the long list actually frees our mental and emotional energy.

We reclaim that energy not by minimizing how much we have to do, but by being very clear about what needs to be done. When tasks are rolling around in our heads, we experience vague dread; distraction also is more tempting than ever because there is no sorting mechanism in our heads. The tasks and feelings of hazy obligation fill our mind, crowding out clear thinking and our ability to get started.

Writing things down right away banishes that mental stress that comes from using our minds for detail storage. Our minds will be better at processing and problem-solving the more we rely on written words to track and store. So our running lists are the homes for tasks that are not on this week's weekly dashboard. The weekly dashboard is home to the tasks that need to happen this week, yet each day more options and obligations present themselves. Running lists are where we capture those incoming tasks that we just don't have room for at the moment.

Each day we work from our daily card and our weekly dashboard; each week we populate a new dashboard. For the most part, the tasks that go on our weekly dashboard don't come from staring at the ceiling and thinking blankly about what we ought to do next. Our weekly dashboard should be filled in as we look over our running lists and our project hub to be sure we're making good choices and not dropping any commitments.

The running list is not an active planner page to refer to throughout the week or midday. It's a holding place. It's the back burner. It's a place to go if you wind up with extra time you want to make the most of. It's the place to refer to as you create your weekly plan. Primarily, it's where you keep those "I should…" thoughts in a home outside of your head.

Often, tasks will wind up on a running list and never get done. We ought not be surprised by this because we're often overcome by ambition, perfectionism, a desire to please, or overcommitment. Seeing all those possible tasks in black and white rather than just sensing them jumbled in our mind's eye allows us to filter them with more clarity and wisdom.

Delete those things you thought last week you really should do, but now you recognize you simply can't worry about anytime soon. If deleting items is too painful, move them to a "someday/maybe" running list instead to review every few months or annually.

When you write tasks on your running lists – and also on your weekly dashboard or daily card – it's best to write them as imperatives. Begin the task with the appropriate verb so it's clear at a glance what exactly to do. A task is something you do. Writing "dishes" is just a placeholder code, not a task, because "Dishes" are things, nouns. To make your list most useful at-a-glance with minimal interpretation and thinking needed, write them with the verb first: "Wash dishes."

Projects are single outcomes that require multiple tasks to finish. They get their own running lists in the project hub, which should be in the same section of your planner as these running lists. For the most part, these running lists are for the one-off, random things we think of doing or for the requests we get that we want to do but can't do right away.

I recognize that keeping running lists might seem nebulous. What do they look like? The reality is that the important part is simply having tasks written down, not having those lists kept in any special template. They can be literal, stream-of-consciousness lists, long and random. They can be categorized in hierarchical patterns with headings or in boxes. Simply choose a method and structure that is visually appealing and understandable to you.

Once we establish a home for all our tasks, no matter the kind, and a pattern of adding to the lists and planning from the lists, we're not worried about forgetting something important. We reclaim our peace of mind when it comes to our tasks and responsibilities. The longer we work the system, the more we trust the process. We also trust ourselves more by increasing our follow-through and becoming trustworthy.

At first, building out your running task list might feel like busywork. As you write down tasks as soon as you think of them, you will certainly feel like you are missing something while also feeling overwhelmed by all the written tasks you aren't doing. However, instead of feeling like you have to figure it out in your head before you get started, you will actually figure out a plan as you stare at and work from a written list.

When our tasks are both written down and written well (by starting with the action we need to take), we can use our minds and attention for creative thinking, problem solving, and focused action.

In your planner

Most of us face the temptation with task management more than any other planning piece to change up styles, apps, or methods, but we must resist the urge. So much time is lost in migrating to new formats that we'd do better to use that time to cross things off our list than write them over again.

Try committing to one type for at least 6 weeks, though 12 is better. You'll then get some use out of the time you put into creating it, and you'll get real daily in-the-muddle experience with what does and doesn't work for you.

If you've tried more than one of these methods, you'll find that they each present the same issues: the lists themselves don't make anything happen automatically and they take regular maintenance to be helpful. No matter how you keep track of your tasks, this will always be true. Put the time into maintenance rather than setting up a new system if you don't want to waste your time planning.

- PREPRINTED PLANNER – Most ready-to-go planners don't have a place for a laundry list of random tasks you'll carry on from week to week and even month to month, so you'll want to establish a section for your running lists in the back notes section. It will go along well with your project hub, so read the next chapter before creating this space in your planner.
- SELF-BOUND PLANNER – Self-bound planners have the added flexibility of pages that can move around. One option you might consider is moving your running task list week by week so it's always directly behind your weekly dashboard. Then it's only ever one page turn away to add extra "I should" thoughts to your planner.
- CLIPBOARD PLANNER – Your running list will likely need to be its own page, somewhere in your stack. To make it easy to find so it's quick to add new tasks to it, you might consider adding a colored flag tab to the bottom of the page so it sticks out a bit no matter where it is in your stack.
- BULLET JOURNAL PLANNER – You probably want to keep your running lists after your weekly dashboard spreads, so you can count backwards to leave space for as many weeks as you hope your notebook lasts you or you can start from the back of the notebook and move toward the center with the running lists and project hub.
- DIGITAL PLANNER – Although you can keep a literal running list in a note app, perhaps as a bullet-point or checkbox list, task management apps are built

for running tasks lists. It is their strength. So decide whether you want everything in one app or whether you want to use each app for what it's best at. The important thing is to be able to add tasks to their designated app right away, so choose an option that makes that fast and easy.

You can find photo examples of running list set ups in each of these kinds of planners at ConvivialPlanner.com – just click "sample pages."

9

YOUR PROJECT HUB

It's true. Planning can be a waste of time. When we make plans that are based on wishful thinking, we're wasting time. If we plan for right now – our current reality, our current responsibilities – then our plan will be helpful to us.

One problem we have with lists is that each task has a similar weight, a similar importance as they march down the page. Not only that, but we often mix tasks, routines, and projects in our lists, so that some things on our lists are not even possible to check off.

Tasks are individual actions you can accomplish in fifteen minutes or less. If it takes longer, it's probably a project – something that takes multiple tasks to accomplish. Tasks belong in our Running List section. Routines are tasks we regularly repeat to maintain our homes and systems. Routines should be on your Routine Details page and possibly on a habit-tracking section of your weekly dashboard.

We might sometimes think of our routines as a project, as a set of tasks to accomplish a goal. The goal would be a clean house, right? But that's not an achievable goal. A clean house requires maintenance, which means it requires routine. It's not a project that can be checked off.

Projects are an undertaking requiring concerted effort, a plan for accomplishing something. Projects have an end; they result in finished products. So housework is not a project because by its nature housework will be repeated. Housework is tending work, caring work, recurring work. The point of housework is to serve and love others and keep our homes in functional condition for the ways God calls us to serve.

By that definition of project, it also becomes obvious that people are not projects, not even the kids whom we are charged with raising. Our job with them is to love, teach, train, disciple, discipline, feed, clothe, and care. God takes our investments and works his will in their lives in a way that will be unforeseen by any of our scope and sequence, vision-mapping exercises.

So we do have projects, but they tend to be fewer and less important than the non-project work in our lives. However, we still need to manage our projects appropriately. When we are able to juggle a few extra projects, we expand our capacity, bless our families and communities, and broaden our own scope of interests.

Because projects have an outcome in mind that requires multiple steps to achieve, we need to track not only those tasks, but also that outcome. When you know why you're working on this project, you can make appropriate decisions on the fly as circumstances develop. A project is a planned set of actions that helps achieve a goal. Thus, projects should always be tied to a goal statement.

If you know the goal of your project, you'll know whether or not the urgent situation in-your-face is more or less important and be able to make better decisions in the day-to-day and the week-by-week. The best way to be sure you know and remember your goal is to write it down and review it. Writing something down and reviewing it separates plans from daydreams.

No matter which kind of a goal you set, I recommend this formulation for writing them out as you choose the steps to achieve the desired outcome (or at least work toward it): "I will x so that y." The x is a clear statement of the project, the y is a succinct statement of the end result, the outcome you're working for. Here are some examples:

- I will refinish the kitchen cabinets so that they are attractively farmhouse-chic.
- I will refinish the kitchen cabinets so that they aren't embarrassing before my mother-in-law comes to visit.

See how the goal of these two statements might keep your focus in a different place? In one, the aesthetic is prioritized, so the project might take longer and be pursued as a creative outlet. In the second, the timeline must be prioritized and the project becomes more about home maintenance.

All the tasks and timeline for a single project should be together on a project reference page rather than scattered on various scrap paper bits and random planner or note pages – or worse yet, in your head. You want to create a project-at-a-glance view and keep your current projects together in a planner hub.

Projects require us to juggle multiple pieces over a certain length of time, so it is best to keep a central "control center" for projects. To begin your hub, brain dump the current projects you have going on in your life right now. Brain dump any projects that are upcoming in the next month. Holidays and birthdays count as projects. Events and crafts-in-progress are projects.

When these projects are written down, we can consciously and without guilt put some on hold by physically removing the papers and filing them for "someday maybe" or even just "next year."

When you have one place for all of them to be named and tracked, you might finally recognize why you feel so scattered. We will discover that we're often spinning projects in our minds that we aren't "counting" as significant enough to matter, yet we let them take up our bandwidth.

In your planner

Write the project name or desired outcome at the top of the page or file. Then write your project statement: "I will x so that y." X is what the project will accomplish and Y is the reason you will work on the project.

The rest of the page will be filled with two things: 1) the information needed to work on the project – important dates, measurements, people's contact info, or whatever else you need; 2) a running lists of project-related tasks. The project page is the home for all the details you need to track and accomplish the project.

Keep this page as the one central location for all notes and information pertaining to that project. Look it over during your weekly review.

- PREPRINTED PLANNER – Your project hubs will most likely live in the back of your planner on the blank or lined note pages. Your project hub is a place for notes on projects, so the notes section is a logical home for it.

- SELF-BOUND PLANNER – You'll want to set up a project hub in your planner after your weekly pages; consider using a flag to mark the beginning of the section or use index tab dividers so you can easily flip to the place you want to be.

- CLIPBOARD PLANNER – Whether or not you want to keep a project hub on your clipboard, depends on how many you have and how bulky you want your clipboard to be. Another option would be to simply keep a current list of projects on the back of your weekly dashboard.

- BULLET JOURNAL PLANNER – You'll likely want to begin your project hub in the back of your notebook. One method is to flip your book so the back is like the front and you can begin filling in projects and notes from the back to the center and weekly dashboards from the front toward the center, and when the two meet, you need a new notebook.

- DIGITAL PLANNER – If you're using a task management app, you may want to use that as your project hub or you can choose a separate app for projects; each project can be a tag or folder, or you can make your project goal statement a task and use subtasks for the required steps. If you're using a notes-based app, I recommend keeping one note per project and beginning each note title with PROJECT.

You can find photo examples of project hubs in each of these kinds of planners at ConvivialPlanner.com – just click "sample pages."

10

YOUR DAILY CARD

After years of trying numerous methods and papers for my daily list and never really being happy with them, I finally landed on a way that has stuck, that helps by its very nature, and that I'm happy to share with anyone who will listen.

Every day, I make a new list on a Post-it note. With such limited space, I'm forced to keep my to-do list short, which is another way of staying realistic. Because humans are limited – in time, in resources, in energy – our to-do list also needs to be limited.

Using a post-it note to make our daily plans helps us remember that not only our time, but even our energy, attention, and abilities are limited. We can't do everything that we might be keeping on some other to do list.

I'm not talking about cramming a full to-do list in minuscule print on a post-it note, either. Our daily to do list begins with a list of the three most important things. Of all the things you will do and want to do, what will "count" as sufficient for the day? If you do those three days, you get to (and really ought to) count the day as a win.

Even such a small planning piece can be used to waste time planning rather than make important decisions ahead of time so our path forward is clear. Most people who begin with a daily top three list end up choosing "extras" for their day rather than the absolute essentials. It's so hard to resist the temptation of idealistic plans, but the daily card is a tool to teach us realism in our planning.

Because we make a brand new card every day, the feedback loop is tight rather than postponed. We get another shot at making a better list right away. It gives us a manageable learning growth curve.

It takes practice and experience to know how to pick a viable, realistic top three. It's not something that anyone else can pick for you. It's something that you have to think about, figure out, try, experiment, iterate, and continually learn from your own experience by evaluating how it went, making observations, and moving forward in light of what you learn. Over time, we make better and better choices.

Your daily card should be populated by looking at your calendar and weekly dashboard. Look over your to-do list for the week and your recurring responsibilities for the day, choose the three most important things you need to do today and write them down. Then do them as early in the day as your schedule (or time budget) allows.

You will, of course, do more in a day than the three things written down on your daily card, but if you start with what's most important, you'll feel better about how you've used your time, and you'll probably even get more done in the long run because you're focused and clear rather than scattered and stressed. You'll see you're spending your time well.

The daily card offers plenty of flexibility. It works for those who are busy Type-A high-energy moms, spinning multiple plates daily, yet it also works for laid-back, spontaneous types as well.

If we identify what's most important, write that down, and make our note-to-self visible, we are more likely to follow through on those items. The exercise of choosing is essential because planning is mostly a thinking exercise.

The daily card reminds us by its very nature to focus on priorities and not to overestimate what we're able to do. Using a daily card also offers three further benefits to our effective planner set up.

First, it promotes flexibility. Every day, we can take stock of our family's needs, our energy, our most pressing obligations, and use our to-do list to put first things first. Some days that might mean project tasks, some days it means completing the homeschool day and that's all, and some days it means dealing with an emergency. Every day, we evaluate and make the best intentional choices we can.

Second, it is manageable. When we're working to increase our effectiveness, it's important to see progress rather than failure. Too often, we only notice what we didn't do in a day, which brings down our attitude and energy. When we complete "everything" on our list of three, we are forced to recognize that we did what needed to be done. We're allowed to call it a good day.

Finally, it is realistic. The limit of 3 reminds us of our finitude. We cannot do all we want to do. We need a to-do list, not a want-to-do list. Choosing 3 tasks forces us to prioritize and focus on what needs to be done rather than what we wish we could do.

It's easy to get distracted by the little things that pile up, but then we end up never getting to those important things that aren't necessarily urgent. This short daily to-do list is where we make sure that we do not lose sight of what's important in our days.

We must make this list every day because every day our time is a little bit different— the time we have available, the kind of energy that we have available — and so we can look at what we actually have by looking at our calendar, looking at our commitments, and choosing what's most important.

In your planner

It's easy to get distracted by the little things that pile up, such that we end up never getting to the important things that aren't necessarily urgent. Our daily cards help us cut through the clutter and focus on what matters.

Be sure you have a visible spot for your daily card, no matter what kind of planer you use.

- PREPRINTED PLANNER – If you use a planner that gives you a page for each day, there is likely a place for your daily top three on each daily spread. That spot is your daily card. If you primarily work from a weekly spread, choose a spot to stick a post-it for your daily card – and that spot doesn't need to be inside the planner! Consider sticking it on the window in front of your kitchen sink or even on the screen of your phone so you return to it throughout the day.
- SELF-BOUND PLANNER – When you choose or create your weekly dashboard, be sure there's a spot to fit a post-it for your daily card. Another option is to cut and hole-punch bookmark sized strips for each day and stick a new one in between your weekly dashboard spread – use the top of the list for the daily card and

the rest for notes and tasks for the day. If you're using a full-size binder, you might consider having one page be your weekly dashboard and the facing page be a daily page with a spot for your top three.

- CLIPBOARD PLANNER – Your weekly dashboard should be the top page you see whenever you glance at your clipboard, so it is the best spot for your daily card. Remember that sticky notes come in many sizes, so you don't have to reserve a 3x3 square if that seems like too much real estate. You might want to use a 2x1$^1/_2$ inch sticky note for your daily card instead.

- BULLET JOURNAL PLANNER – Design your weekly overview with space for a daily card Post-it to come in and out. It can be a bright spot of color on your page, drawing attention with its pop and texture. The more visual and attention-getting the daily card is, the better.

- DIGITAL PLANNER – Although my recommendation would be to keep your daily card as a physical sticky note even if you're otherwise all digital, there are ways to make it work with apps as well. If you're using a note app, add a top section in your weekly overview for your daily top three and write in a new set each day.

You can find photo examples of various types of daily cards in each of these kinds of planners at ConvivialPlanner.com – just click "sample pages."

SECTION 3

How to Use a Planner

"No battle plan ever survives first contact
with the enemy."
—Helmuth von Moltke the Elder

11

USING YOUR PLANNER

It's so tempting to think that the only thing keeping us from being organized is getting the best planner page layout. If we just had that perfect planner, then we'd finally have it all put together.

We spend time setting up or even creating from scratch a once-and-for-all planner that will finally work for us. Then, it doesn't.

Yes, we're missing something. But it's not about the planner; it's about us.

Planning is one thing: thinking ahead, giving ourselves a clear path forward. But doing it is another. Doing it is the actual working of the plan. No matter what planner you have, it won't make your plans happen automatically. Action will always take effort, time, attention, and intention – every day.

We need to not only have a plan, we need to look at it multiple times a day, and we need to then do what it says. Those are the two habits that make planners truly work. With those habits in place, any planner will actually keep us organized.

Putting a planner together is part of using it. Making the lists and writing the notes are good and needed exercises, but the not-so-magic magic is looking at those lists and notes over, updating them, and – most importantly – working from them.

The point is not even to get all the boxes checked off, although that is a wonderful feeling. I almost never do, myself. Instead, the point is to know how to make appropriate and wise choices in the moment as we do the next thing.

We can't do the next thing if we don't know what the next thing is. We can't know if that urgent incoming task is more important than our other projects unless we know what those other projects are and what's next to move them forward.

That's why having a planner with the information and strategies we need written out in black and white is so helpful. With all that written down and given a clear, common-sense home, we are able to review it. Looking it over and using that data to make an informed decision will improve our clarity and effectiveness as we move through our typically messy days.

The planner doesn't make the days less messy. Instead, it helps us cope with and remember to deal with that mess consistently and cheerfully.

Planners take practice

When we buy and arrange our planner, we think we're putting a complete system into place that from here on out will change our lives and make it all work.

When it doesn't, we assume the planner was the problem, or we were a failure – but neither are necessarily true.

There is no single perfect planner. Using a planner is a skill that requires instruction and practice. We don't assume our eight-year-old (or ten-year-old) is a failure when learning multiplication takes days and weeks and many repeated lessons. We know that's exactly what he needs to learn the concept and become increasingly able to do it quickly, without laboring over the process. Before the ease of ability comes, laborious practice time must be invested.

It's the same with the skills of planning.

We learn by doing. We find out what we need written down and what is clutter. We discover what format makes sense to us and whether no-nonsense bullet journalling or colors and stickers and designs will appeal – not which appeals to us when we're at the table with all our supplies, busy making a great planner, but when we're in the midst of a busy average day.

Putting in practice will grow our skills, but it won't mean we'll discover the one best-fit planner we'll be able to use for the rest of our lives. When life changes – and it will – our planner needs will likely need to change and adapt as well. That's not a failure-point but a growing-point. Only machines keep working the exact same day in and day out. Organic, living beings grow and adapt and develop.

Life changes, and the planner we use will change, but the fundamental skills of using a planner do not change. Those skills are three:

- Make a plan.
- Look at it.
- Do it.

It's not complicated, but it is difficult.

Although the hope of a fresh new year often expresses itself in new planners, pretty markers, and a renewed resolve, the reality of life lived with and for other people often undermines our planner-related ambitions. Our renewed resolve must be harnessed to align our attitudes and expectations with reality. One such reality is that life is a maintenance job, not an art project.

Repeating our work, repeating ourselves, repeating our planning processes, is not an indication of futility. It's an indication that we're working with living, growing people in God's world of layered, repeated cycles.

The planner practice process

First, choose a method for how you are going to keep your planner. Changing up your method should be done infrequently. Operate with the motto, "If it ain't broke (much), don't fix it" rather than "The grass is greener over there." Setting up a planner will take a lot of time. It is worth it, but it's not worth the effort to redo it frequently.

Any of the planner types described in this book will work equally well if they are used. You can't mess up. Pick the one that seems most compelling to you and just get started. Give it a fair shot before reevaluating your choice.

Second, set up your planner with the pages and information you'll need to keep it relevant for a decent chunk of time, not just a single week. Write numbers on undated calendar pages. Print several weekly dashboards. Whatever your particular planner needs to hum along for a while, put it together up front.

Now, don't set it up for a full year – you'll want to adapt sooner than that, and most people don't want to carry around 6 or more months of previous or future planning pages anyway. Get started with a month or so first.

Third, regroup and reinvest yourself – without recreating your planner – every week. This happens during the weekly review. Once a week, generally at the end or beginning of the week, you'll go over your lists and notes and plans and pull together a new weekly dashboard with the meal plan, task lists, habit tracking, and notes you need.

A weekly review is a time set aside to briefly look over every single page in your planner so that you know that if you put it in your planner, you will see it and not drop it. The Weekly Review is so important to having a working, effective planner that it gets its own chapter next.

Finally, look at your planner throughout the day. Each morning and evening, go over your daily card and weekly dashboard. Check off what you can, move what you need to, and write a note for the next day. Be sure your planner fits in your purse and make it a habit to grab it as you head out the door. Give it a visible, convenient home in your house where it can stay open to your weekly dashboard page.

Of course, simply seeing and reading your plan isn't enough, though it is necessary. Effectiveness comes by our choices, our actions. The planner doesn't change anything. It informs and reminds us so that we make wise choices.

Wisdom is aligning our actions and affections with what we know to be true. Our plan reminds us of what is true. Wisdom takes that truth and translates it into appropriate action, moment by moment.

Wisdom isn't a place we'll arrive at or status we'll achieve in this life. Instead, it's a path we follow and increase in as we walk by faith, with trust and obedience to the will of God for us in Christ Jesus: our sanctification.

12

YOUR WEEKLY REVIEW

The biggest obstacle we have in working a plan is actually trust.

We don't trust our plan because we fear not being able to be flexible or we doubt our own ability to follow-through.

We know that real life doesn't follow our plans, so our planning time becomes wishful thinking time where we imagine all we could do if things would only go our way. As soon as things don't go our way (like first thing Monday morning), we toss the plan out the window.

We have to do that, because that plan wasn't made for real life.

The weekly review is a time set aside to remind us of what we have on our plates and choose our commitments so we can stay organized.

We take some time and look at the calendar, make fresh to-do lists, decide what our biggest responsibilities are this week, and then make sure those stay in front of our faces so they can get done.

Once we spend some time getting organized, the next step is to stay organized. We can't stay organized without looking at our plans and keeping our systems on track. A weekly review is the key to staying on top of the maintenance that real life requires. Moms need a weekly review just as much as a business executive. We have sports practices, volunteer dates, meals, and so much more we must accomplish in a week. The process of evaluating everything that's upcoming in a calm manner beforehand helps us meet our commitments with peace and preparedness.

Regular review is the absolute key to maintaining a sense of organization. We have to look at our lists to make them happen, and that looking over is called a review. A weekly review sharpens our intuitive focus on our important projects as we deal with the flood of new input and potential distractions coming at us the rest of the week.

If we have a sense of where we are, where we're going, and what we have going on, we'll be able to make better on-the-fly decisions about commitments and responsibilities and ideas that come at us throughout the week. That's one way we stay organized.

But it is hard to discipline ourselves to set aside the time for a weekly review. We are used to scrambling. We just keep on going as one week becomes another without pausing to reflect and set ourselves up for any solid, focused progress. But it is only our own peace of mind and sanity we are sacrificing when we skip a weekly review.

In his productivity classic, *Getting Things Done*, David Allen says that a weekly review is the key to both peace of mind and staying organized. Allen recommends we set aside 2 hours at the end of every week to update lists, do a brain-dump and processing routine, and generally evaluate how things went and what needs to be done next week. This is a time to look at your past calendar, transfer anything you need, look at what's coming up for the next week and the next month, and jot down any notes the overview process inspires.

Instantly, the mom-mind rebels. We do not have a spare 2 hours each week! Allen tries to tell us we will reclaim wasted time by reserving a consistent regular review, and he's not wrong, yet we still cannot commit 2 hours of uninterrupted time to anything as moms at home. There is no office door to close, no phones to hold, no babysitter time to spare.

However, a weekly review does not need to take two hours to be effective. In fact, a weekly review does not need to take even one hour. You can take 15 minutes to get your stuff ready for the week ahead. A weekly review is the key, the linchpin, to being sure that our planner is effective and helpful, not a waste of time.

It is with a regular weekly review that we can keep a clear mind and a sense of relaxed control in the midst of a crazy and full life.

It is precisely because our work at home threatens to deluge and overwhelm us at all hours and every day that we need to carve out a time and space to strategize, to regroup, and to be refreshed.

Our difficulty is not in finding 15-30 minutes for such a review. The difficulty is in choosing to use it for a weekly review instead of zoning out on random internet searches, Pinterest-browsing, or social media scrolling. We must be both savvy and disciplined enough to know the value of sacrificing fake relaxation for the truly refreshing & rejuvenating.

A weekly review is not part of a go-go-go work mode. It is a reserved thinking-time mode where you make sure you have some quiet and you regroup and reassess. I know that can be hard to find. If need be, it is worth getting up half an hour early or staying up half an hour later. It is worth sending the kids outside and using the time to pull things together instead of folding laundry or cruising Facebook.

As moms, we're functioning as managers of our homes – if we want to be savvy and smart, we will take the time to keep up to date and on top of our game. We can't do that moment by moment, so we must carve out thirty minutes or so at the end of the week to pull back and process.

A three-step weekly review

When you sit down with your planner for a weekly review, it helps to have a process list to follow because it is easy to get distracted and sidetracked and waste time.

Gather your planner, calendar, and a notepad for jotting quick notes and brain dumps as you work through your weekly review process. If you have mail or emails that will affect your next week's activities or tasks, have those handy as well.

#1–Flip through your whole planner, glancing at each page.

If you write things down but never look at what you've written, you're not going to trust your planner. You don't have to read every page, but you should flip by and glance at each page, just so you be reminded of what's there.

Look over your calendar closely for the next week, but also check what's coming up in the next three weeks and even the next two months. Is there anything you need to prepare for? Take notes as you read through these big-picture places, don't immediately start filling in your actual task list yet.

With your calendar helping you make smart choices, plan the food for the week – both the menu plan and the shopping list.

Don't draw this process out and make it complicated. Use your meal strategy page to do this quickly. Now is not the time to browse recipes online, but to draw from your previous legwork. As you read the meal strategy pages and pantry master list, use the notepad to sketch your food plan for the upcoming week.

Read over your routine details. How did you do this last week? What's working, what's not working? Now's not the time to change things up, but just to spend a minute thinking about it. What will you work on most this coming week?

#2–Brain dump about your lists and your week

Looking over your lists or your calendar might be overwhelming, or maybe you even came to your planner already overwhelmed. Before choosing priorities and tasks for the week, brain dump what's on your mind and the things you're thinking need to be done.

By brain dumping first, you'll put some space between your reactions to circumstances and your commitment to do what needs to be done. It will give you a process to think through what's going on at least in your head, but also in your life, so you can make good decisions while populating your weekly dashboard.

It's a good idea to use a timer while you brain dump at this stage, setting it for 5 minutes or less. This will ensure you actually do get to the rest of your review and it will rev up your mind by making it work with a time crunch.

#3—Set up your weekly dashboard.

Using your notepad, running lists, and project hub, fill out your plan for the coming week. What will you eat? What will you work on? Where will your time go this week?

Your plan for the week is made of your food plan, your top three tasks, a running list of subordinate tasks, and your routine or habit tracking. Do you have those pieces in place and visible? Is your task list informed by your calendar, notes, and running lists? Don't add an unrealistic number of tasks. Look at your calendar and predict what will be reasonable for the coming week.

Also, look at your previous week's dashboard. How did you do? Do you have tasks that need to move off your current view and onto the running list? Do you need to move last week's tasks onto this week's list? Mark meals that were a hit and those that fell flat so your next meal strategy can be better tuned to your family.

Although it's easy to draw this process out and make it elaborate and consuming, it really can be done quickly, especially if we practice it regularly, use our planners daily, and also set a timer so we remember to focus and not let the time get away from us.

Make an appointment with yourself

A weekly review is a pivotal planner practice for peace of mind.

If possible, set an appointment with yourself to complete your weekly review at a regular time. This will help make it a habit.

The more you do it, the quicker you will become. If your weekly review takes longer than 30 minutes, you're probably doing too much or trying to get everything perfect.

The basic three steps of a weekly review should take 30 minutes or less. Sometime between Friday afternoon and Monday morning is the best time to reserve for this process. Try setting a calendar appointment with a reminder or a phone alarm to help you remember; then use a timer to keep your focus sharp.

Regular review is the absolute key to maintaining a sense of organization. This process might feel like a lot at first, but the more we practice it, the smoother it will become and the less time it will take us – not only because the process is familiar, but because going through the process regularly will prevent the work from piling up.

Not only that, but the more we do it, the more we will get used to the clear mind that comes from having taken care of our business and cleaned up our plans and expectations.

An effective weekly review that actually happens boils down to self-discipline. Ultimately, it's up to us to learn the habit of following through on our decisions. The more we do so, however, the easier it will become over time.

Following through on the weekly review will increase our discipline, focus, and follow-through in every other area as well because it is a time set aside to look over those commitments and make sure we're ready for them.

If you want to work on forming self-discipline, a regular weekly review is a good place to start.

13

REGROUPING WITH YOUR PLANNER

You have done it. I know I have – and too often still do. Life is not going as planned, so we break out the blank paper and start a new plan.

The new plan is not a way to faithfully respond to our current reality, but rather a way to escape into a pretend future reality where our plans will work out.

Turns out we ate all the fudge scraps while making a dessert plate. Clearly time to make a diet plan for January. Turns out we never looked at our planner, even when we left it out on the counter. Clearly we need to buy a new one and start again with a new layout.

Turns out our menu plan failed us – or we failed our menu plan. Food spoiled, we forgot to buy a key ingredient, and we just didn't make what was on the plan. It was supposed to eliminate decision fatigue, but we still scrambled at 5pm. Clearly all we need is a brand new menu plan!

What was the definition of insanity, again?

Right.

We don't need to scrap the plan and start all over. In fact, we need to not do that at all. We need to know how to make plans that aren't merely scratching our productivity itch without moving us forward.

When we trash what we had going (or tried to get going) and spend a bunch of time thinking – or, rather, dreaming – up a new plan, we're indulging in escapist planning.

Escapist planning uses planning as a means to ignore our current reality and enter a pretend reality where things will go our way. In our minds, we skip over right now and start thinking about the future in all its idyllic glory. It is a false glory, however. It's not the glory of duty faithfully performed, of doing the right next thing now. At its heart, it's procrastination. It's daydreaming.

Escapist planning gives us the illusion of organization without any of the payoff in reality. After all, it turns out payoff in reality involves following a plan, and we don't actually want to do that. Instead, we want a plan that will work without us having to work.

And that will never work.

There are three key things we must know so we make plans that are not escapist.

First, when you sit down to regroup, always start with a brain dump. Ask yourself what's not working now, what needs to be done now, what your sticking points are, and what you would like to accomplish.

But don't stop there. Also brain dump about what is working – and don't say that nothing is working. Are people in your house being fed? Something is working, even if the current reality doesn't live up to your imaginary standard.

In fact, go ahead and brain dump what your imaginary standard is. What are the particulars, the specifics, that would make life feel up to snuff for you? Be brave. Write it down. Then look at all that.

Your vision of what you're supposed to make life like is what you're escaping from. No wonder you often want to escape. All of that is overwhelming. I've even had women tell me that the process of brain dumping made them cry.

It might make you cry not only because it's overwhelming, but also because it's cathartic. You've just released all those details that were whirling around in your head, distracting you from moving forward and preventing you from thinking straight. Give those standards and those expectations you're imposing on yourself a cold stare and then cross as much as possible out.

Second, after a brain dump, you can make plans that will help you move forward in your real life and not just pretend that in the future everything will be different. Look at that brain dump and focus on what is working, not what isn't.

Instead of starting your plan over from scratch, build on what's working. Take the next step from where you are towards where you want to be, don't try to imagine where you want to be and build a plan designed to work there.

Progress is made through gradual change, baby step after baby step. Rather than imagining what it would be like to nail the routine and rock the plan, figure out one small piece of the plan you can work at getting consistent at, then add another.

It's not glamorous and it's not flashy or quick, but it is effective, realistic, and doable.

Finally, again, plans only work if you do them. That's the cold, hard truth. It doesn't matter how pretty the planner or how precise the plan – the plan itself does nothing if it does not direct you to take the appropriate action at the appropriate time.

Instead of wasting time on wishful thinking plans, we need to make plans in light of our current reality and use them not as a tool of control against others, but as a tool to control our own moment-by-moment choices – even if that choice is to switch gears and take care of the current urgent, unexpected need.

Our plans should help us make those judgment calls with calm clarity and consistent conviction.

It will take trial & error to figure out a good mix and level of goals, projects, and habit plans for you. You'll likely start out with too many. If you get overwhelmed, choose only 1 or 2 of your projects or habit plans.

Observe. Learn. Tweak. Get started and make those errors so you can get some trial-run results to learn from. Don't get caught stalling out because you're trying to set up a perfect plan from the outset.

The doing is the most important part, but between the making of the plan and the doing it, there must be looking at the plan. We can't work the plan if we don't know what it is. We write it down to remind ourselves, so if we don't look at it, those plans are only wasting our time.

Possibly the next small step of progress you need to make is simply looking at your calendar and your list each morning. It sounds simple and maybe too basic, but take the humble next step: make sure you're looking at those plans you made.

Life happens and sometimes days – or even weeks, maybe months – go by where we don't touch our planner. The longer we go, the less likely we are to pick it back up. When we do pick it up, we need to spend our time cleaning up what we have, reviewing and refreshing it, not creating a brand new planner.

Fresh starts are appealing, but you can make your planner ready for a fresh start by making sure everything is up-to-date and accurate, being sure you have all the essential pieces, and preparing yourself to use the planner daily again.

We will fall off the planner bandwagon. Life will happen. New babies, illnesses, moves, family crises, vacations – any number of things can throw us off our game. However, when that happens we don't need a new bandwagon or a new game. We just need to be willing to pick up where we left off and start again. That's follow-through. That's consistency.

14

PLANNER RESOURCES

Get the 5 free essential planner pages from Simply Convivial so you can get started right away.

- Weekly Meal Planner
- Basic Master Pantry List
- Routine Details
- Weekly Dashboard
- Project Hub

Each of these pages comes in both a full-size sheet and half-sheet format so you can use the planner system you prefer.

Plus, the download pack comes with a handy reference for when to use and review what in your planner so that your work putting it together is not wasted.

You can find them all at ConvivialPlanner.com when you click the "Free templates" button.

ABOUT THE AUTHOR

Mystie Winckler

Mystie Winckler married her high school sweetheart, Matt, at nineteen; together they have five children, two of whom are now in college and three of whom are still being educated at home.

When she's not teaching, checking work, reading, or walking, Mystie publishes articles, podcast episodes, and videos on homemaking without overwhelm or perfectionism on her website, SimplyConvivial.com

Her community, Simply Convivial Continuing Education, is a treasure trove of of mother-mentors engaged in the work at home to which they've been called. If you need camaraderie and mentorship on the path of Christian home management, the not-on-Facebook private community, Convivial Circle, is the place you've been looking for.

Whether we're talking about personal lives, homemaking duties, or homeschooling days, Mystie seeks to return to and live out the motto, *Repent. Rejoice. Repeat.*

Simply ♡ Convivial

REPENT. REJOICE. REPEAT.

homemaking without stress

A t Simply Convivial, Mystie offers mentoring and encouragement for wives and mothers who want to glorify God as they serve their families and communities.

Through articles, podcasts, and YouTube videos, Mystie shows how to manage life cheerfully and live a meaningful life built on solid truth.

Inside Simply Convivial Continuing Education, you'll find instruction, accountability, and camaraderie in your work as a homemaker. Courses, community, and live meetups all serve to point us to Christ first, then toward love and good works as an overflow of gratitude for our great salvation.

Keeping house, managing life, and mothering children is harder than we expected, but also worth more than we can see. Home is a fertile mission ground we can be effective in because it's where God has placed us. We become more effective as we live out the motto: Repent. Rejoice. Repeat.

Be equipped for the mission at SimplyConvivial.com

Made in the USA
Middletown, DE
16 January 2025

69638859R00056